# Idiom of the Week

Heather McDonald

**Primary Concepts**®

Cover Art by Alireza, age 7, Tehran, Iran
©River of Words.

Editors: Stephanie Kruse and Ann Roper
Design: Candace Wesen

©2006 Primary Concepts
P.O. Box 10043
Berkeley, CA 94709

All rights reserved.
Printed in the U.S.A.

No part of this book may be reproduced, stored in a retrieval system or transmitted
in any form or by any means, electronic, mechanical, photocopying, recording, or otherwise,
without the prior written permission of the publisher.

ISBN 978-1-893791-93-0

# Contents

| | |
|---|---|
| Idiom of the Week | iv |
| get the show on the road | 1 |
| bend over backwards | 2 |
| a piece of cake | 3 |
| look up to | 4 |
| call the shots | 5 |
| all thumbs | 6 |
| butterflies in your stomach | 7 |
| hit the ceiling | 8 |
| on thin ice | 9 |
| turn over a new leaf | 10 |
| hold your horses | 11 |
| sing your praises | 12 |
| catch on | 13 |
| up to your eyeballs | 14 |
| on the fence | 15 |
| cut corners | 16 |
| having a ball | 17 |
| toot your own horn | 18 |
| monkey business | 19 |
| like pulling teeth | 20 |
| hit the nail on the head | 21 |
| under the weather | 22 |
| see eye to eye | 23 |
| not my cup of tea | 24 |
| keep a straight face | 25 |
| on pins and needles | 26 |
| hang in there | 27 |
| keep an eye on | 28 |
| give it your best shot | 29 |
| put your foot down | 30 |
| think it over | 31 |
| for keeps | 32 |
| in no time | 33 |
| sneak up on | 34 |
| in the same boat | 35 |
| in a pickle | 36 |
| eat like a bird | 37 |
| pull your weight | 38 |
| raining cats and dogs | 39 |
| cut it out | 40 |
| out of the blue | 41 |
| out of the question | 42 |
| get it off your chest | 43 |
| through thick and thin | 44 |
| a can of worms | 45 |
| off the hook | 46 |
| make light of | 47 |
| in the nick of time | 48 |
| cooking up | 49 |
| keep it under your hat | 50 |
| on top of the world | 51 |
| get on my nerves | 52 |
| cold feet | 53 |
| running out of time | 54 |
| step on it | 55 |
| backseat driver | 56 |
| wrap it up | 57 |
| Index | 58 |

# Idiom of the Week

*Idiom of the Week* is designed to introduce children to idioms so that they will begin listening for them and making them a part of their everyday language. An idiom is a commonly used expression that means something different from what it appears to mean. If something is "a piece of cake," for example, it is not literally a piece of cake; it is something that is easy. The English language is filled with idiomatic expressions, and knowing what idioms mean is an important part of a child's growing knowledge and fluency with the language. Idioms can be especially difficult because there are two levels of meaning: the literal level and the idiomatic level.

Recent research has established that children at the same grade level can have vastly different vocabularies and oral language skills. Some children come from language rich environments where words and their meanings are explained to them daily. Other children's environments are language deprived. Still others speak a language other than English at home. *Idiom of the Week* and its sister book *Word of the Day* (Primary Concepts, 2006) help young children learn words and expressions orally in the primary grades so that they will be able to understand what they read in 3rd grade and above.

Like *Word of the Day,* *Idiom of the Week* is comprised of short oral activities. You can easily combine the two. For example, you could introduce a word each day Monday through Thursday and then finish with an idiom on Friday. There are more than enough idioms in this book to introduce one per week for the entire year. You can work through the book, starting with "get the show on the road" and ending with "wrap it up," or pick and choose lessons.

More important than knowing the meanings of all of the idioms in this book is the goal of appreciating idioms, and to enjoy language in general. Learning about idioms is a great way to help young children begin to see the fun in word play. Idioms in this book appeal to young children's sense of humor and fantasy.

## Getting Started

Take a few minutes each week to introduce the new idiom. Write the idiom on the board for the class to see. Then use the notes on each page to present the idiom to the class.

## Word Story

Children who are familiar with *Word of the Day* will recognize the Wordly family. As you might expect from their name, the Wordly family has a strong vocabulary. Each idiom is introduced with a story about the Wordly family in which the idiom comes into play. Read the word story and then briefly summarize what the idiom means in words the children can understand.

## Talk About It

Ask your students questions, like those listed, that get them to think about the idiom and what it means. Help them use the idiom in different situations. If children use the idiom incorrectly in a response, rephrase their answer so the usage is correct.

Idiom of the Week

©Primary Concepts

## Make It Meaningful

Suggestions are provided for active ways for children to build meaning. Sometimes children act out or draw pictures to show the meaning of the idiom. These short activities are intended to help children remember the idiom in a context they understand.

## Next Steps

After you have introduced the idiom, challenge the children to find a way to use it several times over the next week, either at home or at school. Brainstorm some ways the children can do this.

## Word Jar

After an idiom is introduced, write it on a 3" x 5" card. Keep a large jar in your classroom and put each new idiom in it before you move on to the next one. You may wish to combine the idioms with *Word of the Day* word cards, all in one jar. Periodically, pull out a card and see if the children can remember what the idiom means. Ask them to use it in a sentence.

## Assessment

Assess children's appreciation for idioms by listening to them talk and noting whether they are trying to use idioms in their oral language. You might also challenge the children to be "idiom catchers." Have them listen for these fun expressions and share new ones with the class whenever they discover one. "Idiom catchers" can write their idioms on note cards and add them to the Word Jar.

# 1  get the show on the road

## Word Story

The Wordlys were getting ready to go out for a day at the beach. Everyone was anxious to get started, but it was taking time to get everything packed and ready. "Let's *get the show on the road!*" boomed Mr. Wordly happily.

To *get the show on the road* means to hurry up.

## Talk About It

- Have you ever heard the expression *get the show on the road?* Who said it and what were they talking about?
- How do you think this expression might have come about?
- What type of show would go on the road?

## Do It

When it's time for recess, I'll say, "Let's *get the show on the road!*" That will mean to clean up quickly and line up at the door.

©Primary Concepts

## 2

# bend over backwards

### Word Story

Grandma Wordly *bends over backwards* for her new puppy. She bakes him homemade dog treats, knits him sweaters, and takes him for six walks a day.

If you *bend over backwards* to do something, it means you put more work or effort into the task than anyone would have expected.

### Talk About It

- ✪ What does the meaning of this expression have to do with actually bending over backwards?
- ✪ Can you think of someone who's *bent over backwards* to help you?
- ✪ What would it mean if you said you will *bend over backwards* to study your spelling list this week?

### Act It Out

Let's try to bend over backwards. Get a partner to "spot" you for safety. How far can you go without tipping backwards? It's hard work, right? Just like you *bend over backwards* to do something well.

©Primary Concepts

# a piece of cake

**Word Story**

When the youngest Wordly girl learned to ride her bike, she made it look like *a piece of cake*. It was so easy for her she didn't even wobble or tip over.

When something is easy we sometimes say it's *a piece of cake*.

**Talk About It**
- Name something that's *a piece of cake* for you.
- What does something that's easy have to do with a piece of cake? Any ideas?
- What are some other ways to say that something's easy?

**Tell a Story**

Make up a story that might show how the idiom *a piece of cake* came into use. Sometimes we have no idea where a particular expression came from or what it meant originally, but it's fun to use our imaginations to play with the idea.

©Primary Concepts

**4**

# look up to

### Word Story

One of the oldest Wordly boys is really good at sports and planning games. The younger Wordly children *look up to* him. They admire him and want to be just like him.

If you *look up to* someone, you respect and admire them.

### Talk About It

✪ Think about someone you *look up to*. What is it about them that you admire?

✪ Do you know anyone who *looks up to* you? What characteristics do you have that others might respect?

✪ Is there anyone famous that you *look up to* even though you don't know them personally?

### Picture It

Draw a picture of someone you know and admire. When everyone is ready, each of you will hold your picture above your head and tell who you *look up to* and why.

©Primary Concepts

# call the shots

**Word Story**

Boy, was the middle Wordly girl mad. Her bossy friend said, "I'll *call the shots* in this game!" She wouldn't let anyone else suggest any ideas for how the game should be played.

Someone who *calls the shots* is the leader, and is telling others what to do.

**Talk About It**

- Do you ever get to *call the shots?* With whom? In what situations?
- Can you think of different jobs where someone would be in charge, *calling the shots?*
- If you could *call the shots* here at school, what's one thing you would change?

**Act It Out**

Pretend you are a fire chief *calling the shots* at the scene of a big fire. You need to tell all your firefighters how they can help, where they should go, and what they should do.

©Primary Concepts

# all thumbs

**6**

## Word Story

The Wordlys' uncle is *all thumbs!* Whenever he comes to visit, all kinds of things go wrong. On his last visit, he bumped into Mrs. Wordly's favorite crystal vase and it was smashed to pieces. Then he tried to make scrambled eggs for breakfast, but the carton of eggs slipped out of his hands. Boy, was that a mess!

If someone is *all thumbs,* they are very clumsy and they tend to make a mess of things.

## Talk About It

- What would it be like to have ten thumbs instead of two thumbs and eight fingers?
- Do you know anyone who is *all thumbs?* Tell us about something they've done.
- Have you ever had a clumsy day when you felt as if you were *all thumbs?*

## Do It

Try to pick up your pencil with your thumbs only and draw a circle on paper.

©Primary Concepts

# 7 butterflies in your stomach

**Word Story**

The Wordlys' daughter had *butterflies in her stomach*. She had a piano recital and she was feeling nervous about playing in front of an audience. Her stomach felt all fluttery inside, just as if a flock of butterflies were flying around in there!

If you have *butterflies in your stomach,* it means you have an anxious, nervous feeling inside.

**Talk About It**

- What kinds of situations give you butterflies?
- Do you think grown-ups get butterflies?
- When you have butterflies about something, how do you get through it?

**Write About It**

Use the sentence frame to tell about a time when you felt as if you had *butterflies in your stomach,* and then decorate your paper with butterflies.

I had butterflies in my stomach when I _____.

©Primary Concepts

# hit the ceiling

8

### Word Story

The Wordlys' grouchy next-door neighbor *hit the ceiling* when he found out his front window got broken during the children's baseball game. He was so mad it seemed like he might shoot straight up through the roof.

When someone is really mad, we might say that they *hit the ceiling*.

### Talk About It

- ✪ What makes you so mad you feel as if you might *hit the ceiling?*
- ✪ How does your body feel when you are really mad?
- ✪ Tell about a character in a book or movie who's *hit the ceiling*. What made them so mad?

### Do It

Imagine you're so angry that you are about to shoot straight up and *hit the ceiling*. Show the expression on your face.

©Primary Concepts

# on thin ice

## Word Story

When Mrs. Wordly thinks that one of her children is in a risky situation, or is just about to get in trouble, she often says, "You're skating *on thin ice,* buster." She means that they're putting themselves in a bad position, and that there could be trouble or danger.

If you're *on thin ice,* you are in a risky position, or are heading for trouble.

## Talk About It

- What does it really mean to be on thin ice? What might happen?
- Think about a time when you've been in a risky or uncertain situation. Tell us about it.

## Act It Out

Let's pretend we're stepping out onto an ice-covered lake. We're walking lightly and carefully in case the ice is thin. We're testing for trouble before we get out to the deep part.

©Primary Concepts

# turn over a new leaf

**10**

## Word Story

One of the Wordly boys didn't like to brush his teeth. When he went to the dentist, he was told he had better do a good job or his teeth would be filled with cavities. He decided to *turn over a new leaf* and brush his teeth at least twice every day.

When you *turn over a new leaf,* you decide to do things in a better way.

## Talk About It

- ✪ Have you ever *turned over a new leaf?* What did you change and how?
- ✪ How do you think this expression originated? Might it be talking about plant leaves, or the leaves (pages) of a book? What might make sense?
- ✪ What might you find if you turned over a real leaf on the forest floor?

## Write About It  *Materials: leaf shapes cut from paper*

I'll give each one of you a leaf. On the back of the leaf, write about something that you can do differently, such as brushing your teeth everyday.

©Primary Concepts

# hold your horses

**Word Story**

One idiom Mrs. Wordly uses a lot around the house is *hold your horses!* Everyone is so busy and moving so fast at their house that she often has to remind the children to slow down and be patient.

If someone tells you to *hold your horses,* they want you to stop or slow down, and not be so excited.

**Talk About It**

- Has anyone ever told you to *hold your horses?* What were you doing?
- What if someone was driving a horse and buggy? What would it mean for that person to hold his horses?

**Act It Out**

Pretend you are someone in the old days driving a wagon pulled by a team of horses. You see that the bridge in front of you is broken, so you have to hold your horses.

©Primary Concepts

# sing your praises

**12**

## Word Story

After Mr. Wordly got home from parent-teacher conferences, he told the Wordly boy, "Your teacher was certainly *singing your praises!*" Then he told his son about all the nice things the teacher had to say.

If someone *sings your praises,* they are saying a lot of nice things about you.

## Talk About It

- ✪ What would someone say about you if they were *singing your praises?*
- ✪ What good book have you read lately? *Sing its praises* to us.
- ✪ What wonderful things could we say to *sing the praises* of our town?

## Tell a Story

Sing your own praises. Write down a few great things about yourself, and make up a little tune to go with those words. Who wants to *sing their praises* to the class?

©Primary Concepts

# catch on

## Word Story

On April Fool's Day Mr. Wordly always likes to try to trick his family, but these days they *catch on* fast. They have learned how to spot his jokes a mile away!

If you *catch on* to something, you are able to learn or understand it.

## Talk About It

- Tell about something at school you were able to *catch on* to quickly.
- What sports or activities at home were easy to *catch on* to?
- Have you ever tried to teach someone to do something? Did that person *catch on* quickly?

## Act It Out

Get together with a partner and pretend you're playing catch with a ball. Whenever you catch the ball, call out "Got it!" Just like learning something new—we feel happy and confident when we've *caught on* to how it's done.

©Primary Concepts

# up to your eyeballs

**14**

### Word Story

The Wordlys had just had a party, and now they were *up to their eyeballs* in dirty dishes! It seemed it would take them forever to wash them all.

If you're *up to your eyeballs* in something, you have a lot of it.

### Talk About It

- How much of something would you really need to have to be *up to your eyeballs* in it?
- What are some things we could be up to our eyeballs in? (Halloween candy, homework, good books for summer reading…)
- Think of something good you're *up to your eyeballs* in at home.

### Picture It

Draw a picture of yourself *up to your eyeballs* in something. It could be something you would love, or something you'd rather not have so much of.

©Primary Concepts

# on the fence

**Word Story**

Mr. and Mrs. Wordly were *on the fence* about whether to let their son go camping with his friend for the weekend. They couldn't decide what to do. He would miss his soccer game on Saturday, but camping would be a lot of fun. Hmmm….

If you're *on the fence,* you are undecided about what to do, or which side of a question to support.

**Talk About It**

- Have you ever been *on the fence* about something? What did you end up doing?
- Some people are *on the fence* a lot, others make decisions easily. Which type are you?

**Tell A Story**

Make up a story that might show how the expression *on the fence* came into use. Who is the main character? What problem are they facing? What choices lie on each side of the fence?

©Primary Concepts

# cut corners

**16**

## Word Story

The little Wordlys were supposed to clean their rooms, but what they really wanted to do was go out and play with their friends. They did their work very fast by *cutting corners*. For instance, they pushed toys under the bed instead of putting them away, and they just picked up the biggest scraps and crumbs.

If you *cut corners,* you do a job sloppily and don't spend enough time on it.

## Talk About It

- Do you ever *cut corners?* How, and on what type of work?
- If you were walking around the block and you cut corners, what would that mean? Does that type of cutting corners have anything in common with what the Wordly kids were doing? Explain.

## Do It

Let's walk around the edge of the playground as quickly as possible, but don't *cut corners* to save time! You must walk exactly around the edges.

©Primary Concepts

# having a ball

**Word Story**

The Wordlys were *having a ball* on their vacation. They were having such a great time! They were spending a few days at the beach swimming, looking for shells, burying each other in the sand, and doing all sorts of other fun activities.

If you're *having a ball,* you are having a lot of fun.

**Talk About It**
- Tell us about a really fun time you've had recently.
- Let's list some activities or events that would be *a ball.*
- Where do you think this expression came from? What connection do balls have to fun? Are there any other meanings of the word *ball* that could have a connection to this idiom?

**Picture It**

Draw a picture of some children *having a ball* playing with balls.

# toot your own horn

**18**

## Word Story

The Wordly children are all good artists, but they don't like to *toot their own horns.* They never boast or brag about their beautiful paintings or clever drawings. Mrs. Wordly loves to display her children's work around the house so she can enjoy it every day.

If you *toot your own horn,* you brag about yourself or your abilities.

## Talk About It

- Have you ever heard anyone *toot their own horn?* What were they bragging about?
- Can you *toot your own horn* without bragging? What's your opinion?
- Toot someone else's horn. Tell about someone you know and what they do well.

## Do It

*Toot your own horn* just this once! Tell us about something you do well.

©Primary Concepts

# monkey business

**Word Story**

Sometimes the little Wordly children get into mischief. Their father says jokingly, "Now what kind of *monkey business* are you two up to this time?"

*Monkey business* is mischief.

**Talk About It**
- How do monkeys act? Is *monkey business* a good expression to describe mischievous behavior?
- What type of *monkey business* have you been involved in lately?
- How is the expression *monkeying around* similar to *monkey business*?

**Tell a Story**

Tell a story about what type of *monkey business* the monkeys are up to at the zoo at night when nobody's around. What silly mischief might they be getting into?

©Primary Concepts

# like pulling teeth

**20**

## Word Story

It's *like pulling teeth* to get all the Wordly children to bed at night. It's really hard, because they all get distracted between taking baths, brushing teeth, and putting on pajamas. Also, they all love to read in bed, so it's hard to get them to turn out their lights.

If it's hard to get something organized or happening, we say it's *like pulling teeth*.

## Talk About It

- What would your mom say is *like pulling teeth* at your house?
- Can you think of some situations that would be *like pulling teeth*?

## Write About It

Write a sentence that uses the idiom *like pulling teeth*.

It is like pulling teeth to get me to _____.

©Primary Concepts

# hit the nail on the head

**Word Story**

Mr. Wordly asked the children to guess where the family would be in just one short hour. When they named the family's favorite taco restaurant, he chuckled, "You're absolutely right! You've *hit the nail on the head.*"

If you *hit the nail on the head,* you are exactly right about something.

**Talk About It**

- What is the head of a nail?
- Have you ever used a hammer and nails? What does it mean if you are hammering, and you hit the nail right on the head? What would be the opposite of that?

**Do It**

Let's play a game I call "Hit the Nail on the Head." I'll think of a number between 1 and 100. You take turns guessing, and I'll say "higher" or "lower." When someone guesses my number, I'll say, "You've *hit the nail on the head!*"

©Primary Concepts

# under the weather

**22**

## Word Story

The youngest Wordly girl was feeling *under the weather,* so she came home from school early to rest. She just didn't feel well. Her head was hurting and her muscles were aching.

When you're *under the weather,* you are not feeling well.

## Talk About It

- How do you think this expression came to be? How can you be *under weather?*
- When did you last feel *under the weather?* What were your symptoms?
- What do you do at home when you miss school because you're *under the weather?*

## Picture It

Draw a picture of yourself when you're *under the weather.* Draw weather to match your feelings.

©Primary Concepts

# see eye to eye

**Word Story**

Mr. and Mrs. Wordly almost always *see eye to eye* about family decisions. They usually agree about what rules to set with the children, how to get the kids involved in household chores, and what privileges and consequences make sense.

If you *see eye to eye* with someone, you agree with them.

**Talk About It**
- Is there someone with whom you usually *see eye to eye*?
- Is there someone you rarely *see eye to eye* with?
- What other expressions can you think of about eyes or seeing? (eye on the ball, all eyes, eyes wide open…)

**Do It**

Get a partner and line your faces up so that you are exactly eye to eye.

©Primary Concepts

**24**

# not my cup of tea

## Word Story

The little Wordly boy doesn't like watching television at all. It's just *not his cup of tea.* He would rather be outside or making up his own games than sitting staring at the screen.

If something is *not your cup of tea,* you don't like it very well.

## Talk About It

- ✪ Name three things that are *not your cup of tea.*
- ✪ Tell us about something that is exactly your cup of tea.
- ✪ Where do you think this expression came from?

## Picture It  *Materials: large tea cup shapes cut from paper*

I'll give each of you one of these paper tea cups. On it, draw a picture of something you really enjoy doing; then fill in the sentence frame:

_____ is my cup of tea!

©Primary Concepts

# keep a straight face

**Word Story**

It was practically impossible for Mr. Wordly to *keep a straight face* as Mrs. Wordly tried to trick the children into thinking they were having liver and onions for dinner. He could hardly keep from bursting out laughing.

When someone *keeps a straight face,* they are trying not to laugh or smile as something funny happens.

**Talk About It**
- What do you think *straight face* means? What part of your face are we talking about?
- Have you ever tried to keep a *straight face* as someone tickled you?

**Act It Out**

Pretend someone is sneaking up on your friend to dump a bucket of cold water on his head. You don't want to give the joke away by laughing, so you're trying to *keep a straight face.* How do you look?

©Primary Concepts

# on pins and needles

**26**

## Word Story

The students in the little Wordly girl's class had written silly poems. Their teacher was reading them one by one. Each child was *on pins and needles* waiting for their poem to be read.

If you are *on pins and needles,* you are waiting anxiously for something to happen.

## Talk About It

- ✪ What would it feel like to really be on pins and needles?
- ✪ How do you move when you are anxious or in suspense?
- ✪ What kinds of situations might put people *on pins and needles?*

## Tell a Story

Tell a story about a time when you were *on pins and needles.* What were you in suspense about, or what were you waiting for?

©Primary Concepts

# hang in there

## Word Story

The little Wordly boy was having trouble with his friend. They had gotten mad at each other, and the friend refused to make up. Mrs. Wordly told her son to *hang in there,* and that things would work out soon if he just kept being friendly.

When you *hang in there,* you stay with something and keep trying even if it's very difficult.

## Talk About It

- Why do you think people say *hang in there?* What does the word *hang* mean?
- Tell about a time when you *hung in there.* How did things turn out?
- Can you think of other expressions that use the verb "*hang?*" What do those idioms mean? (hang on, hang up, hang together, hang loose…)

## Do It

Use the monkey bars or another bar on the playground. How long can you *hang in there?* What's your record? Have a friend count for you.

©Primary Concepts

## 28

# keep an eye on

### Word Story

Mrs. Wordly asked her oldest daughter to *keep an eye on* the younger ones while she went to the store. The older girl was used to taking care of her younger brothers and sisters.

When you *keep an eye on* something, you watch it closely and carefully.

### Talk About It

✪ Who most often *keeps an eye on* you after school? Is their eye actually touching you?

✪ If your mom asked you to *keep an eye on* the time, what would she mean?

✪ What else might you *keep an eye on?* (the weather, a pot on the stove, your dog)

### Picture It

Draw a picture of you *keeping an eye on* something. What are you watching so carefully and why? What might happen if you don't watch carefully?

©Primary Concepts

# give it your best shot

**Word Story**

One of the great things about the youngest Wordly boy is that he always gives things his *best shot*. He never cuts corners or does things halfway. He works hard and gives every new challenge his best effort.

When you give something your *best shot*, you are trying your best.

**Talk About It**

- How do you think this expression came to be? What type of *shot* do you think the expression originally meant?
- Tell us about a time when you gave something your *best shot*, even though it was hard or you didn't really want to try it.
- What usually happens when you give something your *best shot*?

**Do It**

Let's pick something from the classroom that we will each try to draw. Once we decide on the object, I will have you *give it your best shot!*

©Primary Concepts

# put your foot down

**30**

## Word Story

Mrs. Wordly felt she just had to *put her foot down* when the children started coming into the house dripping wet. They had been playing a game of tag in the sprinklers; then they began using the front hallway as base. They were dripping all over the floor, and Mrs. Wordly had to tell them to keep the game outside.

If you *put your foot down,* you firmly say that something is not allowed.

## Talk About It

- What does your mom *put her foot down* about? How about your dad?
- What does *putting your foot down* have to do with being firm or strict?
- What do these expressions about feet mean? (best foot forward, put your foot in your mouth, get off on the wrong foot)

## Act It Out

Pretend you are being strict with a little child, and they are not listening. You tell them one more time, and stamp your foot a little bit *(put your foot down).*

©Primary Concepts

# think it over

## Word Story
Mrs. Wordly gave each of her children several options for summer activities to sign up for. She asked each child to *think it over* and let her know their top choice.

When we say we'll *think it over*, we mean we will think carefully about something before making a decision about it.

## Talk About It
- What does *over* mean? Why do we say think it over in this expression?
- What kinds of things do you need to *think over* or decide about?
- How about grown-ups? What types of things do they need to *think over*?

## Tell a Story
Tell us a story about a time that you had a decision to make and needed to *think it over*. What were you deciding about? What were your choices? What did you decide to do?

©Primary Concepts

# for keeps

**32**

## Word Story

The oldest Wordly boy was sorting his old things, trying to get rid of the things he didn't need anymore. He gave his special baseball cards and his bottlecap collection to his little brother who exclaimed, *"For keeps?"*

If you are given something *for keeps,* you may have it as your own.

## Talk About It

- ✪ Have you ever given anyone something of yours *for keeps?* What was it and who did you give it to?
- ✪ What do you have that was given to you *for keeps?*
- ✪ What other expressions do we have that use the word *keep?* (keep your head, keep your word, keep your fingers crossed…)

## Act It Out

Work with a partner. One of you get something small from the classroom, and pretend you are giving it to your partner. Have a little conversation, using the word *keep* as many times as possible!

©Primary Concepts

# in no time

**Word Story**

The Wordlys were so anxious to get to the baseball game that they got ready *in no time*. Everyone got dressed and put on sun screen very quickly, and nobody forgot their hats or gloves!

If something happens *in no time,* it happens very fast.

**Talk About It**

- What kind of special event could make you get ready *in no time?*
- Is there really such a thing as *no time?* Could something happen *in no time?*
- How else could we say that something happened really fast? (lickety-split, in a flash, like that…)

**Do It**

Think of three things you can do *in no time.* Then show us how fast you are.

©Primary Concepts

# sneak up on

**34**

## Word Story

The Wordlys' dog loves to try to *sneak up on* birds at the birdbath. He crouches low, moves slowly and silently through the grass, then pounces at the last second. The birds always fly away, and the dog usually ends up getting wet.

When you *sneak up on* someone, you try to reach them without being seen or heard in order to startle them.

## Talk About It

- ✪ What describing words could we use to talk about someone who was sneaking?
- ✪ Are you any good at *sneaking up on* people? What do you do to surprise them at the end?
- ✪ What animals often *sneak up on* things? Why do they do it?

## Act It Out

Let's show how we look when we're *sneaking up on* someone. How does your body look? How do you move? How do you sound?

©Primary Concepts

# in the same boat

## Word Story

"Well, at least we're both *in the same boat*," Mr. Wordly said to his little boy who had just scraped his knee. Mr. Wordly had an achy knee from playing soccer, so they each knew how the other felt.

If two people are *in the same boat*, it means they are in similar situations.

## Talk About It

- Is there someone who's *in the same boat* as you in some way?
- Can you think of any characters from books that are *in the same boat*? It can be two characters from the same book, or from different books.
- What famous person would you like to be *in the same boat* as? Why?

## Tell a Story

Make up a story about two very different animals who are somehow *in the same boat*. How do the characters meet? What makes their situations similar? Can they help each other?

©Primary Concepts

# in a pickle

## Word Story

The oldest Wordly boy was really *in a pickle.* He had told his mother that he would be home by four o'clock, but he had lost track of time. Now he was going to be in trouble.

When you're *in a pickle,* you're in an unpleasant situation or in trouble.

## Talk About It

- ✪ What's the last *pickle* you've been in?
- ✪ Is there anyone you know who seems as if they're always *in a pickle?*
- ✪ Can you imagine how this expression ever started?

## Picture It

What if you were really inside a sour pickle? Draw a cartoon of yourself in a pickle with just your face sticking out.

©Primary Concepts

# eat like a bird

**Word Story**

One of the younger Wordly children often picks at her food. She eats corn one kernel at a time. She will only eat the tomatoes in her salad, or when she eats cupcakes—she only eats the frosting. Her older brother and sister always tell her that she *eats like a bird*.

If someone *eats like a bird,* they eat very little.

**Talk About It**

- Have you ever watched a bird eat? What type of food do they eat?
- How does a bird eat differently than a dog?
- Do you sometimes *eat like a bird?*

**Act It Out**

With a partner pretend to *eat like a bird;* then pretend to eat like a dog.

# pull your weight

**38**

### Word Story

There was a lot of yard work to be done at the Wordlys' house. The parents had a talk with the children and asked them all to *pull their weight.* If everyone helped out and did their share, the work would go much faster.

To *pull your weight* is to help out as much as you are able.

### Talk About It

✪ Do you *pull your weight* with the chores at your home? Could you be more helpful?

✪ In a big family like the Wordlys, should the little children do equal work? How should the chores be divided?

✪ In a tug-of-war, who *pulls the most weight?* Why?

### Do It

Let's straighten up around the classroom, with everyone *pulling their weight.* What do you see that needs doing? Let's make a list of jobs and do our share.

©Primary Concepts

# raining cats and dogs

**Word Story**

It was *raining cats and dogs* when the Wordlys went to bed. It was cozy to hear the rain on the roof, and to hear it running down the spouts.

If it's *raining cats and dogs,* it's raining very hard.

**Talk About It**
- What do you think dogs and cats have to do with rain? Any ideas?
- What do you like to do on days when it's *raining cats and dogs?*
- What are some other ways we describe rain or weather? (raining buckets, a pea soup fog…)

**Picture It**

Draw a cartoon that would show the idea of *raining cats and dogs.*

©Primary Concepts

# cut it out

**40**

### Word Story

When the Wordly boys were having fun tossing the colorful fall leaves up in the air, their grouchy neighbor came outside and told them to *cut it out*. He didn't want the leaves messing up his lawn.

If you tell someone to *cut it out*, you are asking them to stop what they are doing because it is bothering you.

### Talk About It

✪ Why do you think we use the word *cut* in this expression?
✪ What else might you say to someone to get them to stop what they are doing?
✪ What has someone done lately that you wanted them to stop?

### Act It Out

Let's see if we can make up some hand signals to mean *cut it out*. What different ideas can we come up with?

©Primary Concepts

# out of the blue

**Word Story**

One day, *out of the blue*, Mrs. Wordly's van just quit working. There was no warning at all. Nothing had been going wrong. She was just driving down the road and the car "clunk, clunk, clunked" to a stop.

Something that happens *out of the blue* comes without warning or is unexpected.

**Talk About It**
- Think of a movie or book where something happened *out of the blue*. How did this unexpected event make the story more interesting?
- What do you think *the blue* is in this expression?
- What other words or idioms might we use to describe something happening without warning? (suddenly, all of a sudden, all at once…)

**Tell a Story**

Tell us a story about something that happened to you unexpectedly—*out of the blue*. When did it happen? How old were you? Who were you with?

# out of the question

**42**

## Word Story

When the middle Wordly girl asked her mother if she could sleep over at a friend's house on a school night, Mrs. Wordly said that it was *out of the question.* There was no way she would allow it.

When something is *out of the question,* it will not even be considered.

## Talk About It

- ✪ What things are *out of the question* or definitely not allowed at your house?
- ✪ What behaviors are *out of the question* at school?
- ✪ What other expressions can we think of that start with out of…? (out of time, out of it, out of the blue…)

## Picture It

Draw a picture of something amazing you might wish for as a birthday gift, but that would be *out of the question.* Maybe it would be too expensive, or too hard to care for, or too big…

©Primary Concepts

# get it off your chest

**Word Story**

When something is bothering the littlest Wordly girl, her mother can always tell. Mrs. Wordly encourages her daughter to tell about her worry or fear as a way of *getting it off her chest*. Once she has shared her problem, she feels better.

When you tell someone what's bothering you, you *get it off your chest* and usually feel better.

**Talk About It**
- Have you ever felt so worried that your chest or body felt crushed by a big weight?
- Who do you like to talk with to *get things off your chest?*

**Act It Out**

Sometimes when you're worried or scared, you feel as if a big weight is on your chest. Get a partner and have that person pretend to lift the weight off your chest. How do you feel?

©Primary Concepts

# through thick and thin

**44**

## Word Story

The youngest Wordly girl had a best friend she had known since she was a toddler. They did everything together. They stuck together *through thick and thin.* If one girl had a problem, the other would help her through it.

*Through thick and thin* means during good times and bad.

## Talk About It

✪ Who are the people that will stick by you *through thick and thin?*

✪ Where do you think this expression came from? What do you think *thick and thin* mean?

## Picture It

Draw a picture of someone who is with you *through thick and thin.*

©Primary Concepts

# a can of worms

**Word Story**

Mr. Wordly certainly opened *a can of worms* when he bought the family tickets to a baseball game without asking everyone if they were available. Mrs. Wordly had to cancel activities for some of the children, rearrange carpools, and come home early from her job to make it all work.

When someone causes a big messy problem that's hard to fix, we say they've opened *a can of worms*.

**Talk About It**

- What would it look like if you opened a real can of worms? How does this compare to a messy problem that's hard to control?
- Have you or anyone you know ever opened *a can of worms?* Tell us about it.

**Tell a Story**

Tell a story about a real can of worms or about a problem that is *a can of worms*. Then we'll have to decide whether you are using an idiom or not.

©Primary Concepts

# off the hook

**46**

## Word Story

The oldest Wordly girl was supposed to baby-sit for her younger brothers, but Mr. and Mrs. Wordly's plans got cancelled. "Well, I guess you're *off the hook!*" her mother told her. Now she could go to the movie with her friends instead.

*Off the hook* means you are freed from blame or an unwanted responsibility.

## Talk About It

- What do you think this expression originally referred to? Who was on the hook? What happened?
- Have you ever been blamed for something you didn't do? Then what really happened is discovered, and you were *off the hook.*

## Act It Out

Get a partner. One of you is the fisherman, and one is the fish. The fish is caught, but it wiggles around enough to finally get off the hook.

©Primary Concepts

# make light of

## Word Story

When the oldest Wordly boy started a band with some of his friends, he took it very seriously. His brothers and sisters laughed and joked about how often the band was practicing, and how mad they got if they were interrupted. "Don't *make light of* this! It's very important to me," their brother shouted.

If you *make light of* something, you don't treat it seriously.

## Talk About It

- Is there anything that is very important to you but which others in your family *make light of*?
- Do you think this expression has anything to do with heavy and light?

## Picture It

Draw a picture of something that is important to you that you wouldn't want others to *make light of*.

©Primary Concepts

# in the nick of time

**48**

### Word Story

Mrs. Wordly thought she was going to be late getting to the airport, but she arrived just *in the nick of time*. Another minute and she would have missed her plane!

*In the nick of time* means just in time, or just at the right moment.

### Talk About It

- ✪ What do you think a *nick* is? Would a nick be a long or a short time?
- ✪ Are you usually early for things, or do you show up just *in the nick of time?*
- ✪ What are some other time-related expressions? (just in time, at the last minute, in a second, time is ticking, out of time, time will tell…)

### Act It Out

Pretend you are getting to school just *in the nick of time*. Hurry into your chair so you're not tardy!

©Primary Concepts

# cooking up

**Word Story**

Mrs. Wordly's birthday was coming, and it was clear Mr. Wordly was *cooking up* some kind of surprise. He was acting kind of funny, and making a lot of secret phone calls. Mrs. Wordly could hardly wait to find out what he was up to.

If you are *cooking up* something, you are concocting or making plans.

**Talk About It**
- Who have you *cooked something up* with lately?
- What do you think I have *cooked up* for you for the rest of the school day?
- How does the meaning of the expression *cooking up* relate to actual cooking?

**Tell a Story**

How would you *cook up* a fun day? Make a list of "ingredients" for the perfect day.

©Primary Concepts

# keep it under your hat

**50**

### Word Story

The Wordlys bought their oldest daughter something special for her birthday. They told the younger children about the gift, but asked them to *keep it under their hats*. They didn't want them to tell, because then the surprise would be spoiled before the big day.

To *keep it under your hat* means to keep something secret or private.

### Talk About It

- Have you ever been asked to keep a secret? How does that feel? Are you good at *keeping it under your hat?*
- What kinds of things could you keep hidden, or secret, under a real hat?

### Do It   *Materials: any type of hat*

Let's take turns pretending there is something under our hat. When you wear the hat, think of a secret object. We'll ask you yes or no questions to try to figure out what you're *keeping under your hat!*

©Primary Concepts

# on top of the world

### Word Story
The little Wordly boy was *on top of the world!* Summer vacation was coming up soon. He couldn't wait to swim, play with his friends all day, and read in the sun.

When you're *on top of the world,* you're feeling extremely happy.

### Talk About It
- How would you feel if you could really be sitting on top of the world?
- When is the last time you felt as if you were *on top of the world?*

### Picture It   *Materials: a globe*
Draw a circle to represent the world; then draw a picture of yourself *on top of the world.* Fill in the sentence frame:

I am on top of the world because _____.

# get on my nerves

**52**

## Word Story

The Wordly children told their mother that their grouchy neighbor really *gets on their nerves.* They aren't allowed to step on his grass, and if they make too much noise he will come out and scold them. They feel as if he's always watching, waiting to catch them at something he disapproves of.

If I say you *get on my nerves,* it means you irritate or annoy me.

## Talk About It

- ✪ What are nerves?
- ✪ What kinds of things really *get on your nerves?*
- ✪ Do you ever get on anyone's nerves? Whose, and what do you do that annoys that person?

## Act It Out

Work with a partner. Pretend one of you is doing something to get on the other's nerves. Practice a few times; then show the class.

# cold feet

**Word Story**

One of the Wordly girls is such a fast swimmer she decided to enter a swimming contest. The day of the race she woke up with *cold feet*. She was afraid she would not be brave enough to race, but when she got to the swimming meet, her *cold feet* disappeared. She won first place!

If you get *cold feet,* you get fearful of doing something.

**Talk About It**

- Have you ever gotten *cold feet?* What happened?
- Have you ever been in a situation where your feet felt very cold?
- How is the expression *cold feet* like the feeling of having actual cold feet?

**Act It Out**

Imagine you have ice cubes on your feet. You are about to do something and you are getting cold feet. Pretend to kick off the ice cubes and do what it is you need to do.

©Primary Concepts

# running out of time

**Word Story**

The Wordlys were *running out of time* to get to the concert. It was taking them all such a long time to get ready; and now they might be late!

If you're *running out of time,* you are almost late.

**Talk About It**

- ✪ What do you *run out of time* for?
- ✪ How many of you were *running out of time* to get to school this morning?
- ✪ What does it mean to be *in time* or *on time* for something?

**Do It**

When we are cleaning up for the day, I will remind you that we are *running out of time.*

©Primary Concepts

# step on it

## Word Story

Yesterday Mrs. Wordly got in her car to go to work and discovered the car wouldn't start. She had a very important meeting to get to, and she just couldn't be late. She asked her husband to drive her to work. When she got in his car, she said, *"Step on it!"* She wanted him to hurry and get her to the office fast.

When you say *step on it,* you mean to hurry and not waste any time.

## Talk About It

- How do you think the expression *step on it* relates to cars and drivers? How do you make a car go faster?
- Describe a time when you were in a particular hurry to get somewhere. Why were you so anxious to get there?

## Do It

I'll tell you when it's almost recess time. Then let's really *step on it* to clean up the classroom and get out to have some fun.

©Primary Concepts

# backseat driver

## Word Story

The oldest Wordly daughter is such a *backseat driver!* Whenever she is riding in the car with her mom or dad, she's constantly giving them advice: turn here, don't follow so closely, stoplight coming up. It sometimes gets a little annoying taking direction from someone who doesn't even have a driver's license yet!

A *backseat driver* is a passenger who is always telling the driver what to do.

## Talk About It

- Can someone really drive from the backseat?
- Do you ever give your mom or dad advice while they're driving?
- Are the drivers in your family annoyed by *backseat driving?*

## Act It Out

Get a partner and arrange your chairs one in front of the other. Pretend the person in the front is driving and the backseat passenger is nagging them and correcting them about what to do. Pretend to be a *backseat driver.*

# wrap it up

**Word Story**

We've had a lot of fun this year exploring idioms and expressions with the Wordlys, but now it's time to *wrap it up.* This is our last page. We hope you enjoy livening up your language with colorful idioms as much as the Wordlys do!

When you *wrap it up,* you finish something.

**Talk About It**

- Why do you think *wrap it up* means to finish something?
- Have you been using more colorful expressions in your language since you've met the Wordlys?
- What is one of your new favorite idioms? Can you remind us what it means? What do you picture in your mind when you hear that expression?

**Picture It**

Draw a picture of one idiom you remember from this book, or one that you've heard somewhere else. We'll bind our pictures together into a class book.

©Primary Concepts

## Idiom of the Week
## Index

a can of worms . . . . . . . . . . . . .45
a piece of cake . . . . . . . . . . . . . .3
all thumbs . . . . . . . . . . . . . . . .6
backseat driver . . . . . . . . . . . . .56
bend over backwards . . . . . . . . .2
butterflies in your stomach . . . . .7
call the shots . . . . . . . . . . . . . . .5
catch on . . . . . . . . . . . . . . . . .13
cold feet . . . . . . . . . . . . . . . . .53
cooking up . . . . . . . . . . . . . . .49
cut corners . . . . . . . . . . . . . . . .16
cut it out . . . . . . . . . . . . . . . . .40
eat like a bird . . . . . . . . . . . . . .37
for keeps . . . . . . . . . . . . . . . . .32
get it off your chest . . . . . . . . .43
get on my nerves . . . . . . . . . . . .52
get the show on the road . . . . . . .1
give it your best shot . . . . . . . . .29
hang in there . . . . . . . . . . . . . .27

having a ball . . . . . . . . . . . . . . .17
hit the ceiling . . . . . . . . . . . . . .8
hit the nail on the head . . . . . . .21
hold your horses . . . . . . . . . . . .11
in a pickle . . . . . . . . . . . . . . . .36
in no time . . . . . . . . . . . . . . . .33
in the nick of time . . . . . . . . . .48
in the same boat . . . . . . . . . . . .35
keep a straight face . . . . . . . . . .25
keep an eye on . . . . . . . . . . . . .28
keep it under your hat . . . . . . . .50
like pulling teeth . . . . . . . . . . .20
look up to . . . . . . . . . . . . . . . . .4
make light of . . . . . . . . . . . . . .47
monkey business . . . . . . . . . . . .19
not my cup of tea . . . . . . . . . . .24
off the hook . . . . . . . . . . . . . . .46
on pins and needles . . . . . . . . .26
on the fence . . . . . . . . . . . . . . .15

on thin ice . . . . . . . . . . . . . . . .9
on top of the world . . . . . . . . .51
out of the blue . . . . . . . . . . . . .41
out of the question . . . . . . . . . .42
pull your weight . . . . . . . . . . . .38
put your foot down . . . . . . . . . .30
raining cats and dogs . . . . . . . .39
running out of time . . . . . . . . .54
see eye to eye . . . . . . . . . . . . . .23
sing your praises . . . . . . . . . . . .12
sneak up on . . . . . . . . . . . . . . .34
step on it . . . . . . . . . . . . . . . . .55
think it over . . . . . . . . . . . . . . .31
through thick and thin . . . . . . .44
toot your own horn . . . . . . . . . .18
turn over a new leaf . . . . . . . . . .10
under the weather . . . . . . . . . . .22
up to your eyeballs . . . . . . . . . .14
wrap it up . . . . . . . . . . . . . . . .57

©Primary Concepts